Grizzly Bears

Patricia Kendell

HODDER
Wayland

An imprint of Hodder Children's Books

Alligators Chimpanzees Dolphins Elephants
Gorillas Grizzly Bears Leopards Lions
Pandas Polar Bears Sharks Tigers

 © 2003 White-Thomson Publishing Ltd

Produced for Hodder Wayland by White-Thomson Publishing Ltd

Editor: Kay Barnham
Designer: Tim Mayer
Consultant: Harry Reynolds – Grizzly Bear Research Biologist,
Alaska Department of Fish and Game; President of the
International Association of Bear Research and Management
Language Consultant: Norah Granger – Senior Lecturer in Primary
  Education at the University of Brighton
Picture research: Shelley Noronha – Glass Onion Pictures

Published in Great Britain in 2003 by Hodder Wayland,
an imprint of Hodder Children's Books.

The right of Patricia Kendell to be identified as the author of this
Work has been asserted by her in accordance with the Copyright,
Designs and Patents Act 1988.

All instructions, information and advice given in this book are
believed to be reliable and accurate. All guidelines and warnings
should be read carefully and the author, packager, editor and
publisher cannot accept responsibility for injuries or damage arising
out of failure to comply with the same.

Photograph acknowledgements:
Heather Angel 15; Bruce Coleman 9, 10 (Bruce Coleman Inc),
11, 12 & 32, 14, 1 & 19 (Johnny Johnson), 16 (Joe McDonald);
FLPA cover & 8 (M Hoshino), 13 (Gerard Lacz), 28-29 (Thomas
Mangelsen), 7 (Mark Newman), 23, 25 (Minden Pictures); NHPA
26 (Andy Rouse); Oxford Scientific Films 18 (Bennett
Productions), 27 (Bob Bennett), 20 (Matthias Breiter), 4, 22
(Daniel Cox), 24 (Frank Huber), 17, 21 (Marty Stouffer); Science
Photo Library 5 (William Ervin), 6 (Leonard Lee Rue III).

British Library Cataloguing in Publication Data
Kendell, Patricia
  Grizzly bears. – (In the wild)
  1. Grizzly bears – Juvenile literature
  I. Title II. Barnham, Kay
  599.7'84

ISBN: 0 7502 4139 X

Printed in Hong Kong by Wing King Tong Co. Ltd.

Hodder Children's Books
A division of Hodder Headline Limited
338 Euston Road, London NW1 3BH

Produced in association with WWF-UK.
WWF-UK registered charity number 1081247.
A company limited by guarantee number 4016725.
Panda device © 1986 WWF ® WWF registered trademark owner.

The website addresses (URLs) included in this book were valid at
the time of going to press. However, because of the nature of the
Internet, it is possible that some addresses may have changed, or
sites may have changed or closed down since publication. While
the author and Publisher regret any inconvenience this may cause
readers, no responsibility for any such changes can be accepted by
either the author, packager or the Publisher.

Contents

Where grizzly bears live

Most of the grizzly bears left in North America live in Alaska or in the Rocky Mountains.

Their close **relative**, the black bear, also lives in North America. There are six other different types of bear around the world.

Baby grizzly bears

Between one and four bear **cubs** are born in a **den**
dug by their mother, or in a safe place such as a cave.
At first, the tiny, helpless cubs cannot see or hear.

They drink rich, creamy milk from their mother
so they can grow big and strong.

Looking after the cubs

The cubs leave the den when they are four months old. But they stay close to their mother.

Grizzly mothers **protect** their cubs from other
large bears and animals such as these wolves.

9

Growing up

The grizzly cubs learn to keep out of danger. Some cubs will climb up a tree to keep safe.

Their mother teaches them what is good to eat and where to find it. The young bears also learn **survival skills** by play-fighting with one another.

Leaving home

When they are two or three years old,
it is time for the young grizzlies to
leave their mother.

The first year alone can be difficult
and some young bears go hungry.

Food

Grizzly bears eat as much as they can during the warm months of the year, when there is a lot of food to be found. They eat roots, nuts and insects.

Berries and meat are great treats.
This grizzly has caught a tasty fish.

Hunting

Grizzly bears have a good sense of smell.
This helps them to find and kill animals
hidden in the grass.

Sometimes they steal a meal from other
animals. An adult grizzly is powerful
enough to chase off a pack of wolves.

Meeting other bears

Grizzlies mostly live alone. But they meet together
where there is a lot of good food to eat or fish to catch.

In the summer, male grizzlies look for a **mate**.

The winter sleep

During the winter, the grizzly bear does not eat. It lives off the fat in its body which it made by eating a lot in the summer months.

The bear makes a den in the ground
where it can sleep all winter.

Waking up

The bears start to wake up when the spring days become longer and warmer. Soon there will be lots of food for the hungry bears.

When it is very hot, the bears will rest in
the daytime and look for food at night.

23

Threats...

The places where grizzly bears live are being taken over by people. They build houses, roads and grow food in these places.

Hungry bears come near to where people
live, looking for food. A very hungry grizzly
might kill farm animals.

...and dangers

Sometimes, frightened people shoot grizzly bears.

Some bears are killed on the roads.

Helping grizzlies to survive

It is important that grizzly bears have enough space of their own. They need to find their own food, away from where people live.

Understanding more about what grizzlies
need will help more of them to survive
in the future.

Further information

Find out more about how we can help grizzly bears in the future.

ORGANIZATIONS TO CONTACT

WWF-UK
Panda House, Weyside Park,
Godalming, Surrey GU7 1XR
Tel: 01483 426444
Website: http://www.wwf.org

Alaska Department of Fish and Game
Fairbanks, 1300 College Road, Fairbanks,
AK 99701-1599, USA

BOOKS

Bears and Pandas: Michael Bright, Lorenz Books 2000.

Bears (Endangered! Series): Horton Casey, Benchmark 1996.

Bears: Claire Robinson, Heinemann 1997.

Bears in the forest: Karen Wallace, Walker 2001.

Glossary

WEBSITES

Most young children will need adult help when visiting websites. Those listed have child-friendly pages to bookmark.

http://www.panda.org/kids/wildlife
WWF's virtual wildlife site has information about why brown bears are endangered and what is being done to save them.

http://www.animal.discovery.com
This site has a photo sequence called 'growing up grizzly', a quiz and video about grizzly bears.

http://nwf.org/kids
This National Wildlife Federation website has information, games and virtual tours about bears.

cubs – young animals, in this case, young grizzly bears.

den – a wild animal's home.

mate – male bears find a female bear to make babies with.

protect – take care of.

relative – someone in the same family.

survival skills – things that the bears learn how to do to help them to live in the wild.

Index